15-Minute Meals

35 Quick and Delicious Healthy

Recipes that are easy to cook

by Kayla Langford

INTRODUCTION

When it comes to nurturing your body and minds, nothing is greater than to cook your food from your own kitchen, served and prepared with love. This book is excellent for anybody who is pressed for time to menu plan or may just want that quick meal.

These are 15 minutes recipes, unless otherwise indicated, a few could take the cook up to 20 minutes. This is a great book to have for delicious, nutritious and healthy quick recipes. They don't require tons of ingredients, but taste great and are quick to fix so they fit into your busy home or work life.

All of the recipes have the full ingredients and preparation. This cookbook is for everyone, from the one who loves cooking and trying new things, to the one who doesn't have a lot of time. Quick and easy to prepare! It is a "must. Let's Get Started!

TABLE OF CONTENTS

#1 SHRIMP WITH SWEET CORN

This is a great simple meal for dinner which is served with corn, sliced bell pepper, and onion. Use fresh shrimp in a combination of three types of crushed chili powder; cook the cut shrimp on low flame.

Ingredients:

- 3 1/2 teaspoons brown sugar
- 2 teaspoons crushed chili powder
- 1 teaspoon another chili powder (ancho, cayenne, or paprika)
- ½ teaspoon regular salt
- 1 1/2 pounds prepared large shrimp
- 5 teaspoons oil
- 1/2 cup cut onion
- 1/2 cup cut red bell pepper
- 2 teaspoons minced garlic
- 2 teaspoons minced ginger
- 1 packet frozen corn
- 1 1/2 tablespoons vinegar
- 1/2 cup cut green onions

Preparation:

1. Mix the 2 teaspoons brown sugar, chili powder, other chili powders, and 1/4 teaspoon regular salt in a little dish. Dredge the shrimp with the spice mixture.

2. Heat 1 tablespoon oil in a big non-stick pan over average high flame. Add 1/2 cup chopped onion, cut bell pepper, garlic, and cut ginger to skillet; cook 4 minutes. Mix rest of 1 1/2 tsp. brown sugar and corn to pot; cook 4 minutes, stir frequently; add vinegar. Boil 30 seconds. Put the corn mixture in a big bowl; mix in rest of 1/4 teaspoon salt and 1/2 cup chopped fresh onions.

3. Put 2 tsp. oil in the skillet over average high flame. Put shrimp in the pot and cook 3 minutes or until tender, turning once. Serve with sweet corn mixture.

#2 CHICKEN AND CASHEWS

This is a delicious recipe with chicken and an Asian sauce which has cashews, cut ginger, sweet honey, and sesame oil. You can use this as first course with steamed rice.

Ingredients:

- 3 tbsp. soy sauce
- 2 tbsp. waterless sherry
- 4 tsp. corn flour
- 1 pound chicken breast, cut into small pieces
- 1/2 cup fat-free chicken broth
- 1 tbsp. honey
- 2 tsp. sesame oil
- 3/4 cup sliced onion
- 1/2 cup sliced celery
- 1/2 cup cut red bell pepper
- 1 tbsp. fresh ginger
- 2 garlic pieces, crushed
- 1/2 cup sliced onions
- 1/4 cup cut unsalted cashews

Preparation:

1. Mix 1 tbsp. soy sauce, dry sherry, 2 tsp. corn flour , and diced chicken in a big bowl; Mix well. Mix rest of 2 tbsp. soy sauce and 2 tsp. corn flour, chicken broth, and honey in small bowl.

2. Put 1 tsp. of oil in a big pan over medium-high flame. Add chicken to the pan; Cook 3 minutes and remove from pan. Add 1 tsp. oil in pan. Add the onion, celery, and sliced bell pepper to the pan; Cook 2 minutes ;add ginger and garlic and sauté for 1 minute;   Mix in soup mixture. Boil for 1 minute, stirring continually. Remove from heat. Stir in the fresh onions and cashews.

#3 CHICKEN WITH MIXED FRUIT SALAD

Chicken, water melon, walnuts and any fruit you love can mix with salad greens for a cool summer salad. Use your preferred summer fruits in this mixer as you wish.

- Makes: 4 servings

Ingredients:

- 1/4 cup low fat sour cream
- 3 tbsp. fruit seasoned vinegar
- 4 tsp. brown sugar
- 1 1/2 tsp. poppy seeds
- 1/4 tsp. salt
- Newly minced pepper, to flavor
- 8 cups salad greens
- 2 cups diced cooked chicken breast.
- 2 cups sliced melon or other fruit
- 1/4 cup cut walnuts which is toasted
- 1/4 cup feta cheese

Preparation:

1. Mix sour cream, white vinegar, brown sugar, poppy seeds, salt and pepper in a big bowl until smooth.

2. Combine the mixed greens with the sour cream mixture.

3. Add the diced chicken, water melon, fruits, walnuts and feta. Add 1 tablespoon of the dressing.

Tips & Notes

- **Tips:** Sauté the diced chicken breast in 1 tbsp. olive oil; add seasonings of choice such as garlic salt, pepper.

- To sauté chopped nuts, use a small skillet on low heat; add 1 tsp. oil-add the nuts and cook tile slightly browned, about 2-3 minutes.

#4 CHOP STEAK AND MUSHROOM SHERRY SAUCE

Cubed steaks are an economical meal for busy week nights. Serve with mashed potatoes and broccoli.

- Makes: 4 servings

Ingredients:

- 4 cube steaks.
- 3/4 tsp. crushed red pepper
- 1/2 tsp. salt
- 3 tbsp. olive oil
- 8 pieces sliced mushrooms, about 1/2 cups
- 1 large shallot finely diced
- 1 tbsp. all-purpose flour
- 1 tsp. sliced fresh basil or 1/4 teaspoon preserved
- 1/2 cup waterless sherry
- 1/2 cup condensed low sodium beef soup
- ½ cup low fat sour cream

Preparation:

1. Season steaks with 1/2 tsp. crushed pepper and salt. Put 1 tbsp. oil in a large nonstick fry pan over medium heat. Sauté the steaks, turning once, until brown; cook 1 to 2

minutes on each side on medium heat. Remove the steaks to another plate and cover to remain warm.

2. Add 1 tbsp. oil to the saucepan. Put mushrooms, shallot and rest of the 1/4 teaspoon chopped pepper. Cook and stir until the mushrooms are golden brown, cooking for 3 to 4 minutes. Dredge with all-purpose flour and cook, stir for 1 minute. Mix basil, dry sherry and beef soup; bring to a boil and cook. Stir continuously, about 3 minutes. Remove from the heat; add the sour cream. Put the steaks into pan and cover with the sauce.

Tips & Notes

- **Ingredient Note:** Sherry is a kind of refreshed wine which is from southern Spain. Don't use the cooking sherry which is also found in many supermarkets; it may be high in sodium. In its place, add dry sherry that is sold with other refreshed wines at liquor store.

#5 GINGER-STEAMED FISH WITH SAUCE

This sauce is a soy-based sauce. Just add fresh ginger and garlic to it. Shoya is used most widely in many hotels. The dish is prepared with a red snapper, which is a tender, flakey, type fish. Makes: 6 servings

- Total Time: 20 minutes

Ingredients:

Fish:

- 6- 5-ounce red snapper filets; skinned- or any type flakey white fish

  6-1/4 inch thick fresh peeled ginger sauce
- 1/4 cup crushed peeled garden-fresh ginger
- 1/4 cup chopped garlic
- 1/4 cup sesame seeds
- 2 tablespoons canola oil
- 2 tablespoons toasted sesame seeds
- 1/4 cup reduced sodium soy sauce
- 2-3 scallions, finely sliced

Preparation:

1. Place about 1 to 2 inches of water in a large pan so that it can hold a bamboo steamer. Place a heatproof bowl in

both of the steamer carriers. Keep 3 servings of fish on every plate with a slice of fresh ginger on top. Stack the carriers, cover and place over the boiling water. Steam the prepared fish for 7 minute, depending on thickness of fish.

2. How to make sauce: mix the crushed ginger, garlic and roasted sesame seeds in a small dish. Heat the canola oil in a medium pan over medium- high heat. Add the ginger blend and cook. Stir until fragrant, about 1 minute. Add sesame oil; allow mixture to get hot. Add the soy sauce carefully and cook for 1 minute.

3. Place the fish to a large platter. Remove the slices of ginger. Pour the sauce over the cooked fish and serve with scallions.

#6 EASY SWEET AND SOUR CHICKEN

A very delicious dish best served for weekend dinner. It is quick and easy to make.

- Makes: 4 servings

Ingredients:

- 4 tablespoons all-purpose flour
- 1/2 tea spoon garlic powder
- 1/2 tsp. salt
- 1/2 tsp. crushed black pepper
- 1 pound skinless, boneless chicken breasts, cut into 1-inch cubes
- 3 tbsp. oil
- 3 celery ribs, cut
- 2 green bell peppers, diced
- 1 onion, diced
- 1/2 cup tomato ketchup
- 1/2 cup lemon juice
- 1/2 cup crushed pineapple with juice
- 1/3 cup packed brown sugar

Preparation:

1. Mix garlic powder, flour, salt, and crushed black pepper in a small dish.

2. Coat and roll chicken cubes in the seasoned flour mix

3. Add 2 tablespoons vegetable oil in a pan over medium-high temperature.

4. Cook and stir chicken in hot oil until no longer pink in the middle and liquids get clear, 9 to 10 minutes; take out and set on the side.

5. Again add 1 tablespoon vegetable oil in the same pan over medium heat.

6. Prepare and add celery, green bell peppers, and chopped onion in oil until tender, about 4-5 minutes.

7. Whisk tomato ketchup, lemon juice, crushed pineapple, and brown sugar in a dish; add to the skillet; bring to a boil.

8. Cook and mix chicken and vegetables in sauce until heated throughout, 3 minutes.

#7 FLUFFY PANCAKES

These pancakes are fantastic and easy to make. Top with strawberries and whip cream for a delicious meal, anytime of the day!

Servings: 8

Ingredients

- 3/4 cup milk
- 2 tbsp. white vinegar
- 2 tbsp. white sugar
- 1 cup all-purpose flour
- 1 tea spoon baking powder
- 1/2 tsp. salt
- 1/2 tsp. baking soda
- 1 egg
- 2 tbsp. melted butter
- Cooking spray

Preparation:

1. Mix the milk with vinegar in a medium bowl and set aside for 4-5 minutes to sour.
2. Mix the flour, baking powder, sugar, baking soda, and salt in a big mixing bowl. Beat egg and butter into sour milk. Add the flour combination into the wet ingredients and mix until lumps are gone.

3. Heat a big pan over medium heat, and add cooking spray. Pour 1/4 cup full of batter in the pan, and cook until bubbles show. Flip and cook until it becomes browned on the other side.
4. Top with strawberries and whipped cream.

#8 BLACK BEAN CATFISH WITH GARLIC

This is a great low calorie and healthy recipe that uses flavorful black bean sauce. Serve with broccoli or rice for a delicious, quick meal.

- 4 servings
- Total Time: 20 minutes

Ingredients:

- 1/4 cup all-purpose flour

- 1 pound catfish filets, dried and cut into 4 slices

- 1/2 teaspoon garlic powder

- 1/4 teaspoon salt

- 1 tbsp. plus 1 teaspoon oil

- 1 tbsp. black bean garlic sauce

- 1 tbsp. finely chopped scallion

- 1 tbsp. rice vinegar

- 1 tbsp. water

- 1/8 tea spoon crushed red pepper

Preparation:

1. Put flour in a medium dish. Season catfish with garlic powder and salt. Dredge the catfish in the flour.
2. Heat 1 tablespoon oil in a big non-stick skillet over medium heat .Add the fish to skillet, turning once- cook until golden brown and continue to cook, about 4-5 minutes each side.
3. In the meantime, mix the remaining 1 tbsp. oil, black bean garlic sauce, 1 tablespoon of vinegar, scallion, and water along with crushed red pepper in a small dish.
4. Serve fish with this sauce and enhance with more scallions to taste.

Tips:

Black bean with garlic sauce, a spicy, salty sauce used in Chinese meals, is prepared with black soy beans, garlic and rice wine. It can be found in the Asian-foods section of most supermarkets or in Asian markets.

#9 BLACK BEAN WITH SALMON PANFRY

This is a tasty and simple meal using salmon and black bean garlic sauce. It's pan-fried which allows a delicious crusty coating. Serve on bed of rice and steamed veggies.

Makes: 4 servings

- Total time: 20 minutes

Ingredients:

- 1/4 cup water
- 2 tbsp. rice vinegar
- 2 tbsp. black bean garlic paste or sauce
- 1 tbsp. wine or dry sherry
- 2 tsp. cornstarch
- 1 tsp. crushed red pepper flakes
- 1 tbsp. oil
- 1 pound salmon , skinned and cut into 1-inch cubes
- 12 ounces bean sprouts
- Scallions ,sliced

Preparation:

1. Mix water, rice vinegar, black bean garlic paste, rice wine, cornstarch and red pepper in a small bowl.
2. Pour oil in a large, non-stick skillet over medium high heat. Add salmon and cook, gently stir, for 2-3 minutes. Combine bean sprouts, sliced scallions and the sauce mixture. Cook and continue stirring, until the bean sprouts are cooked down and tender, 2 to 3 minutes.

Tips & Notes:

- **Notes:** Black bean-garlic sauce is sauce used in Chinese cooking. It is made from black soybeans, garlic and rice wine. You can get it in the Asian-foods part of any supermarket or in an Asian market.
- **Tip:** to skin a salmon filet: Place salmon fish on a fresh cutting board, skin side down. Begin at the tail end, slide the knife-edge of the long knife between the fish flesh and the skin, and hold down with your other hand. Slide the blade along at a 35° angle, separating the fillet from the fish skin without cutting in the middle.

#10 GREEK SALAD WITH SARDINES FISH

The Greek salad contains different, tangy, spicy essentials. Cucumber; feta, tomato, fresh olives and lemony dressing are added. Fresh or canned sardines may be used. Lightly season them with salt and crushed pepper and sauté in a light virgin olive oil if desired.

- Makes: 4 servings
- Total Time: 20 minutes

Ingredients:

- 3 tablespoon lemon juice
- 2 tablespoon olive oil
- 1 piece garlic, crushed
- 2 teaspoon dried oregano
- 1/2 teaspoon minced pepper
- 3 average size tomatoes cut into large pieces
- 1 large cucumber, cut into big pieces
- 1 15-ounce can peas
- 1/3 cup feta cheese
- 1/4 cup finely cut red onion
- 2 tablespoon sliced fresh olives
- 2- 4-ounce cans sardine fish in olive oil or water.

Preparation:

1. Mix lemon juice, olive oil, chopped garlic, ground pepper and oregano in a medium bowl, until well mixed. Add tomatoes, cucumber, peas, feta, cut onion and olives. Toss to mix them.
2. Serve the salad on each of 4 plates and top with sautéed sardines. Serve them with desired garnish.

#11 GRILLED CHICKEN WITH SALSA

This is a great recipe for summer grilling or you can sauté the chicken breast on stovetop. The pineapple-tomato salsa adds a tangy topping to the meat or with tortilla chips on the side.

- Makes: 4 servings
- Total Time: 20 minutes

Ingredients:

Salsa:

- 1/2 cup diced red peppers
- 1/3 cup diced red onions
- 1 -2 cups diced fresh pineapple
- 3-4 tomatoes, diced
- 1/3 cup lime juice
- 3 tbsp. minced cilantro
- 1 small jalapeno, seeded and diced

Chicken:

- 4 boneless and skinless chicken breasts
- 1 tablespoon olive oil

- 1/2 teaspoon salt
- ¼ teaspoon pepper, to flavor
- ¼ cup lemon juice
- 2 tbsp. lime juice
- 2 tbsp. orange juice
- 1 tsp. sugar

Preparation:

1. To make salsa: combine salsa ingredients in bowl until mixed well. Refrigerate until ready to serve.
2. To make chicken: Marinate the chicken with the olive oil, lemon, lime and orange juices, sugar ,salt and pepper and place in Ziploc bag. Refrigerate for 3-4 hrs. Cook on grill with medium heat, about 6 minutes per side. Serve with the salsa.

   Preserve and refrigerate the salsa up to 2-3 days.

#12 CORN MEAL CRUSTED CHICKEN NUGGETS WITH BLACKBERRY MUSTARD

Mixing chicken preparation with cornmeal gives the chicken pieces crunch without using a deep fryer. Blackberries added with stone ground mustard create a slightly sweet-and-savory sauce. It can be served with broccoli and carrots for a delicious and healthy weeknight meal.

- Makes: 4 servings
- Total Time: 20 minutes

Ingredients:

- 1 cup fine diced fresh blackberries
- 1 -1/2 tablespoon whole ground mustard
- 2 teaspoons honey
- 1 pound chicken breast tenders, cut in half
- 1/2 tsp. salt
- ¼ tsp. ground pepper
- 3 tbsp. corn meal
- 1 tbsp. olive oil

Preparation:

1. Smash blackberries, mustard and honey in a small bowl until it looks like a sauce.
2. Season chicken pieces with salt and pepper. Put cornmeal in a medium bowl, add the chicken and mix. Remove the remaining cornmeal.
3. Heat the oil in a large nonstick fry pan over medium-high temperature. Lower the temperature to medium and cook the chicken, turning the chicken once or twice, until it browns and is cooked, 5 to 7 minutes. Serve the fried chicken nuggets with the berry- mustard sauce.

#13 COOKED SALMON WITH CREAMY SAUCE

Easy to make salmon is tender with a lemon-garlic sauce. Anyone can make it as a meal. Serve with peas or asparagus and brown rice.

- Makes: 4 servings

Ingredients

- 1 pound middle-cut salmon fish fillet, peeled and cut into 4 parts
- 1 cup white wine
- 2 teaspoons olive oil
- 1 big shallot, minced
- 2 tablespoons lemon juice
- 1 tsp. lemon pepper
- 1/4 cup low- fat sour cream
- 1/4 tsp salt
- 1 tablespoon shallot, minced
- Dash of hot sauce

Preparation:

1. Lemon Sauce-Heat a large skillet over medium-high heat. Add the wine, lemon juice, shallot. Cook for 3-4

minutes. Add the salt, lemon pepper, dash of hot sauce and simmer on low about 2-3 minutes. Stir in the sour cream until blended. Keep warm till fish is cooked.

2. Fish-In a large pan, add the olive oil and heat on medium-high. Add fish and sauté, 4 minutes on each side until browned.

3. Serve with the lemon sauce.

Tip:

To remove skin from a salmon fillet: Put skin part down. Hold and start from the tail end. Make slit with a sharp knife between the fish skin inner and the outer, holding down tightly with other hand. Gradually drive the knife-edge at a 35° angle and isolate the fillet from the skin in this way.

#14 GRILLED CHICKEN WITH VEGETABLES

This dish gives a classic taste of summer by grilling the different vegetables like red bell pepper, fresh eggplant, garden fresh zucchini and red tomato. It is crowned with grilled brown chicken; it is a cool main course for summer. Serve over rice.

- Makes: 4 servings

Ingredients:

- ½ cup olive oil
- 1/3 cup honey
- 1-1/2 cup balsamic vinegar
- 1 teaspoon salt
- Olive oil or cooking spray
- 1 red fresh red bell pepper cut into strips
- 1 little eggplant, cut into rounds
- 1 fresh zucchini sliced
- 4 red tomatoes, cut
- 1 large red onion, cut into rounds
- 4 Chicken breasts, boneless, skinless
- 1/4 teaspoon ground pepper
- 2 cups rice, prepared as directed on mix

Preparation:

1. Combine the 1st 3 ingredients in bowl and mix well. Add chicken and coat. Cover and chill for 2-3 hrs.
2. Remove chicken from the marinade and grill at medium-high heat. Add salt and pepper to taste. Grill each side of chicken about 5 minutes. Transfer to platter.
3. Spray each side of fresh bell pepper, round cut eggplant, zucchini slice, tomato slice and onion rings with cooking spray. Now grill vegetables, rotating once or twice, until cooked, approximately 4 minutes each side of the pepper, 3 minutes each for the eggplant and sliced zucchini and 2 minutes for each side of the tomatoes and onion.
4. Prepare the rice as directed on package.
5. Dice the grilled veggies and serve with rice.

Notes:

You can prepare extra marinade for the veggies if desired and mix with the diced veggies for extra flavor.

#15 SUMMER VEGETABLE CREPES

Crepes are delicious in this flavorful recipe-easy to fix for busy weeknights. These are filled with ricotta cheese, green beans, fresh zucchini and sweet corn and topped with sour-cream and chive sauce. One should place a wax paper beneath each crepe as you prepare it. You can serve with salad.

- Makes: 4 servings

Ingredients:

- 1/3 cup reduced-fat sour cream
- 1/2 cup fresh chives, chopped
- 3 tbsp. low-fat milk
- 2 tsp. lemon juice
- 3/4 tsp. salt
- 1 tbsp. olive oil
- 2 cups zucchini, chopped
- 1 1/4 cups green beans, chopped
- 1 cup fresh corn kernels
- 1 cup part-skim ricotta cheese
- 1/2 cup shredded Monterey Jack cheese
- 1/4 tsp. ground pepper
- 4 -9-inch ready-to-use crepes

Preparation:

1. Mix sour cream, ¼ cup chives, milk, lemon juice and 1/4 tsp. regular salt in a little bowl until combined.
2. Heat the oil in a large non-stick pan on a medium-high heat. Mix chopped zucchini, green beans and sweet corn and cook, stir, till beginning to brown, 7-8 minutes. Reduce heat to low; stir in ricotta cheese, Jack cheese, the 1/4 cup chives, the rest of 1/2 teaspoon regular salt and pepper. Cook and stir gently, till the cheese melts. Remove from the heat.
3. To roll crepes, put on a piece of foil paper or wax paper. Put one-fourth of the vegetable and cheese mixture down the middle of the crepe. Gently roll the crepe around the filling. Serve the crepes topped with 2 tbsp. of the sauce; add more chives if needed.

Tips:

Ready-to-use crepes are easy and convenient. Find them in the produce section or refrigerated breads.

#16 SHRIMP & VEGETABLES WITH CREAMY GARLIC PASTA

This is a mix of garlic and yogurt sauce. It is also combined with boiled pasta, pieces of cooked shrimp, garden fresh asparagus, peas and fresh bell pepper which is a great summer meal. It is served with sliced cucumber and tomatoes mixed with lemon juice and olive oil.

- Makes: 4 servings

Ingredients:

- 6 ounces spaghetti
- 12 ounces raw shrimp, cut into pieces(peeled and deveined)
- asparagus, cut and finely sliced
- 1 red fresh bell pepper, finely sliced
- 1 cup frozen or fresh peas
- 3 cloves garlic
- 1 1/4 teaspoon salt
- 1 1/2 cups yogurt(plain)
- 1/4 cup chopped parsley
- 3 table spoons lemon juice
- 1 table spoon olive oil

- 1/2 tea spoon pepper
- 1/4 cup roasted nuts

Preparation:

1. Boil a big pot of water. Add spaghetti and boil 2 minutes less than according to package instructions. Add the shrimp, cut asparagus, fresh bell pepper and the peas and cook until the pasta is cooked and the shrimp are properly cooked, about 2-4 more minutes. Drain the water.
2. Mash garlic and salt in a big bowl and until it forms a paste. Stir in yogurt, parsley, lemon juice, olive oil and bell pepper. Add the pasta and mix. Sprinkle the roasted nuts on it.

Tips & Notes:

Ingredient Note: If shrimp cannot be managed correctly it can harm the nearby ecosystems. So try to search for that shrimp which is certified by a self-regulating organization. If you cannot find certified shrimp, select wild-caught shrimp.

Tip: To roast nuts, put in a little dry pan and roast over medium- low flame, stir, about 3-4 minutes.

#17 STEAK WITH BABY POTATO AND GREEN BEAN

This is a healthy quick meal with meat or chicken. Serve with a salad.

- Makes: 4 servings

Ingredients:

- 1 pound baby potatoes
- 12 ounces green beans
- Cooking spray
- 1 pound steak, prepared and cut crosswise
- 1/4 teaspoon steak seasoning
- 1/4 teaspoon black pepper
- ¼ teaspoon salt
- 1 tablespoon miso
- 1 tablespoon rice wine vinegar
- 1 teaspoon minced ginger
- 1 teaspoon sugar
- 1/2 tea spoon sesame oil
- 2 table spoons olive oil
- 1/3 cup fine cut scallions
- 1/2 tea spoon toasted sesame seeds

Preparation:

1. Stick each potato with a knife, put in a microwave-safe dish and lightly cover with some plastic wrap. Microwave on high 4 to 6 minutes or till the potatoes are tender. Microwave and cook green beans as directed on the package.

2. Heat a skillet over medium- high heat. Cover with cooking spray. Season the steak with the steak seasoning and pepper; cook 4 minutes each side or to your desired doneness. Remove it to a chopping board.

3. While steak is being cooked, combine miso, vinegar, ginger, sugar and sesame oil in a bowl. Add in vegetable oil.

4. Cut potatoes in half, then chop steak into 1/4-inch pieces. Divide potatoes, cut steak and green beans among four plates. Top with the dressing. Add the scallions over the steak and roasted sesame seeds on the sliced potatoes for garnish.

#18 CHICKEN CORDON BLEU PASTA

This is a tasty recipe for the entire family-serve with fresh fruit salad for a healthy meal.

Ingredients:

- 10-12 oz. penne pasta
- 2 cups heavy cream
- 8 oz. cream cheese
- ½ tsp. garlic salt
- ½ tsp. onion powder
- 1 1/2 cups shredded cheese (Swiss, mozzarella, or parmesan)
- 2 chicken breasts (cooked and diced-can use rotisserie chicken from market for convenience)
- ¾ cup diced ham
- 1 cup frozen or fresh peas
- Bread crumbs

Preparation:

1. Cook the pasta as directed on package. Drain off the water.
2. Heat the cream cheese on medium-low on stove, until melted. Stir in the heavy cream; add onion powder and garlic salt to taste. Stir in 1 cup cheese until smooth.

3. Layer pasta noodles, chicken, and ham in 9x13 pan; pour sauce on top and sprinkle with ½ cup shredded cheese and bread crumbs.

4. Bake at 350 degrees for 15-20 minutes till heated through.

#19 CHICKEN WITH TOMATOES AND OLIVES

Olives adds salty flavor to this dish which contains only 5-ingredients. It is served with greens on the side. You can add fresh vegetables like red or orange bell peppers, cucumber, or scallions. This dish can include many items you have in your pantry or fridge.

Ingredients:

- The 5 ingredients:
- 4 chicken breasts (boneless, skinless) Chicken can be grilled or sautéed in skillet.
- 1 cup cherry or grape tomatoes(cut in half)
- 3 tablespoon oil and vinegar dressing
- 20 olives-halved
- 1/2 cup feta cheese

Preparation:

1. Preheat grill to medium- high flame. Season the chicken with 1/4 teaspoon salt and 1/4 teaspoon ground black pepper. Put the chicken on the grill after spraying rack with cooking spray. Grill it for 5-6 minutes per side or till chicken is cooked. Cover and keep warm.

2. Mix the tomatoes, 1 1/2 table spoons prepared dressing, and cut olives in a medium pan over medium heat, and cook for 2 minutes or till the cut tomatoes become slightly soft and the ingredients are heated. Brush the chicken with the rest of 1 1/2 table spoons prepared dressing. Cut each chicken breast into small slices. Add ¼ of the tomato mixture to sliced chicken. Top with 2 tablespoons of the feta cheese.

#20 CHICKEN AND VEGETABLE SOFT TACOS

This is a flavorful meal that is quick and easy to fix. This dish uses fresh vegetables, combined with the salsa Verde for a convenient meal. A dab of hot sauce adds some kick to the mixture!

- Makes: 4 servings

Ingredients:

- 2 tsp. oil
- ¼ tsp salt
- 1 tsp cumin
- ¼ tsp pepper
- ¼ tsp crushed red pepper flakes
- 1 cups chopped onion
- 1 cup chopped zucchini
- 1 cup fresh corn kernels
- ½-1 cup salsa Verde
- 12 oz. chicken breast tenderloins
- 1 cup low-fat sour cream
- 1 cup shredded Monterey-Jack cheese
- 4 flour tortillas

Preparation:

1. Combine the pepper, salt and cumin, stirring well. Heat the oil in large skillet on medium-high heat. Sprinkle spice mix on chicken; add chicken to pan and sauté about 3 minutes. Add onion, corn, zucchini and sauté 2 more minutes until chicken is done.
2. Stir in salsa; cook 2-3 minutes till the liquid almost evaporates.
3. Spoon about ¾ cup chicken mixture in the center of tortilla; sprinkle with ¼ cup shredded cheese. Top with sour cream.
4. Roll tortilla.

#21 CHICKEN SHAWARMA

Shawarma is a dish using garlic flavored meat or chicken which is served on pitas. You can get this item on the table in 15 minutes. Use any excess yogurt and add lemon sauce to it on pita bread.

- Makes: 4 people serving

Ingredients:

Chicken:
- 2 tablespoons lemon juice
- 1 teaspoon curry powder
- 2 teaspoon olive oil
- 3/4 teaspoon salt
- 1/2 teaspoon cumin
- 3 garlic pieces, minced
- 1 pound chicken breast, cut into strips (boneless, skinless)

Sauce:
- 1/2 cup Greek yogurt -plain
- 2 tablespoons tahini
- 2 teaspoons lemon juice
- 1/4 teaspoon salt

- 1 garlic piece, minced
- Rest of ingredients:
- Cooking spray
- 4 pitas
- 1 cup chopped lettuce
- 8 tomato slices

Preparation:

1. Heat the grill to medium high heat.

2. To make chicken, mix first 6 ingredients in a medium bowl. Add chicken to the bowl and mix well. Let mixture stand at room temperature about 15 minutes.

3. To make sauce- Mix yogurt and next 4 ingredients and stir with whisk.

4. Add 2 chicken strips onto each of 8 skewers. Put it on a grill rack covered with cooking spray. Now grill it for 5 minutes on both sides or until fully cooked.

5. Put pitas on the grill rack and grill it for 1 minute on both sides or until it is lightly toasted. Put 1 pita on each plate; put 1/4 cup lettuce and 2 sliced tomatoes on each plate. Add 4 sliced chicken pieces to each plate. Add sauce as topping to each serving.

#22 SALMON NOODLE DISH

This 20 minute dish uses plenty of healthful and metabolism- increasing ingredients. The salmon and avocado are filled with healthy fats, and the fried noodles and mixed vegetables are great in fiber. The asparagus are the silent idol of this plate, giving an extensive collection of important vitamins.

- Prep Time: 5 minutes
- Cook Time: 15 minutes
- Yield: Makes 2 servings

Ingredients:

- 4 ounces noodles (whole-wheat)
- 5 ounces asparagus, sliced into thirds
- Cooking spray
- 1 salmon fillet(skinned) cut into 8 pieces
- 1 tablespoon toasted sesame oil
- juice of 1-2 limes (3 tbsp. juice)
- 1/4 teaspoon salt
- 1/4 teaspoon pepper
- 4 ounces cucumber-cut into small pieces
- 1/2 small avocado, cut into pieces

Preparation:

1. Prepare the noodles in the boiling water till they become soft, about 8 minutes. Transfer noodles to strainer; add asparagus to the same boiling water. Cook well for about 2 minutes. Rinse with cold water.

2. Heat a skillet over medium- high flame. Use the cooking spray to cover lightly. Cook the salmon fish filet until done, about 3 minutes per side.

3. Prepare the dressing: Mix sesame oil, lime juice salt and pepper in little bowl. Combine the noodles, asparagus, and dressing in a bowl.

4. Add the cucumber and cut avocado; Mix to coat. Add the salmon pieces.

#23 BLACK BEAN AND CHICKEN

This is a quick and easy meal when you are busy or tired-uses ingredients that cuts the preparation time down. Using quick cook rice package also saves time.

- Yield: 4 servings

Ingredients:

- 4 cups cooked rice
- 2 cooked chicken breasts-cut into small pieces (can use rotisserie chicken from market to save time)
- 1 15oz. can black beans, drained
- 1 jar salsa
- ½ cup shredded cheddar cheese
- 1/4cup sour cream
- 15 corn tortillas

Preparation:

1. Prepare the rice according to package directions.

2. Combine ½ cup salsa and black beans in microwave-safe bowl. Cook about 2 minutes on high until hot-stir to combine.

3. Put 1 cup cooked rice in each bowl

4. Top rice with black bean/salsa mixture, chicken pieces, shredded cheese and sour cream.

5. Serve with tortilla chips and salsa on side.

#24 PANFRY SALMON WITH PINEAPPLE SALSA

Lean protein is vital to any healthy dish. And there's no healthier source of lean protein than salmon fish, which contain heart-healthy fats (omega 3).

- Yield: serves 4
- Time:20 min

Ingredients:

- 1 cup diced, fresh pineapple
- 2 tablespoons diced red onion
- 2 tablespoons diced cilantro
- 1 tablespoon rice vinegar
- 1/8 tea spoon crushed red pepper flakes
- Cooking spray
- 4 salmon fillets
- 1/2 teaspoon salt

Preparation:

1. Mix first 5 ingredients in a bowl; set aside.

2. Heat a non-stick skillet covered to medium- high flame; coat with cooking spray. Season the fish with salt. Fry fish for 4 minutes on both sides or until it is flakey. Cover with salsa.

#25 BEAN AND POTATO SALAD WITH SHRIMP

You can make the vinaigrette dressing while the potatoes and beans are cooking. This is a healthy, delicious meal, low in calories and fat!

Ingredients:

- 1 pound potatoes (can use fingerling potatoes or other small potatoes)
- ½ pound thin beans, cut and
- 2 teaspoon Dijon mustard
- 2 ½ tablespoon cider vinegar
- 1 tablespoon olive oil
- ¼ teaspoon salt
- ¼ teaspoon pepper
- 2 tablespoon chopped dill
- ¾ pound shrimp, cooked, peeled and deveined(about 15)
- ¼ cup toasted pecans

Preparation:

1. Put potatoes in sauce pan; cover with water so that it is 3 inches above potatoes. Bring to boiling then simmer potatoes until they become tender, about 6-7 minutes. Add green beans; cook the beans until they are crisp and tender for 3 minutes.

2. While cooking potatoes, mix vinegar, olive oil, salt, crushed pepper, Dijon mustard and 1 tablespoon dill; stir to mix well. Put the dressing aside.

3. Put shrimp and small potatoes and bean mix on a large plate; sprinkle with dressing. Serve with pecans. Garnish with chopped dill.

#26 BOILED BROCCOLI & FETA OMELET

This meal can be eaten anytime of the day, not just for breakfast. Use either fresh or frozen broccoli. Both will work fine. The cheese adds extra punch of flavor.

- Total Time: 10 minutes
- Yield: 1 serving

Ingredients:

- Cooking spray
- 1 cup chopped broccoli
- 2 large eggs, beaten
- 2 tablespoons crumbled feta cheese
- 1/4 tea spoon dill
- 2 slices bread, toasted

Preparation:

1. Heat a nonstick pan over medium flame. Coat the pan with cooking spray. Add broccoli and cook about 3 minutes.

2. Mix the egg, feta cheese, and dry dill in a small dish. Add the egg mixture to the pan. Cook about 4 minutes; Cook about 2-3 minutes or till cooked properly. Eat with toast.

#27 CHOCOLATE BANANA BITES

Ingredients:

- 2 tablespoons semi- sweet chocolate chips
- 1 small banana cut into 1-inch slices

Preparation:

1. Put chocolate chips in a heavy plastic bag or small microwave-safe bowl. Heat on high at 1 minute or till chocolate is melted. Cover banana slices in chocolate.

#28 BBQ MOIST BURGERS

BBQ moist burgers are tender and tasty; it is a great

Ingredients:

- 1 pound ground beef
- 1 garlic piece, minced
- 1/2 teaspoon paprika
- 1/4 teaspoon ground cumin
- Pinch of salt
- 1/4 teaspoon crushed black pepper
- 4 slices onion, grilled
- 1/4 cup barbeque sauce
- 4 seeded buns, toasted

Preparation:

1. In medium bowl, mix together garlic, crushed paprika, and cumin.

2. Shape the ground beef into 4 patties-season with salt and pepper on both sides

3. Heat grill to medium- high flame to cook; cook burgers about 5-6 minutes per side until done; baste with barbeque sauce on each side. Garnish with preferred toppings and buns.

#29 RICE SALAD

This 15-minute dish is easy to prepare and is a flavorful, healthy dish for your family. Serve with a lemon vinaigrette if desired.

- Yield: 4 servings

Ingredients:

- 2 tablespoons olive oil
- 1/2 sweet onion, thinly sliced
- 1 15 oz. can chickpeas, drained and washed
- 1/2 teaspoon ground cumin
- 1/4 teaspoon salt
- ground black pepper
- 3 cups brown rice, cooked to package directions
- 1/2 cup sliced dates
- 1/4 cup chopped mint
- 1/4 cup chopped parsley

Preparation:

1. Heat the oil in a large nonstick pan over medium-high flame. Add onion, and cook about 4-5 minutes or till onion browns.

Remove from heat, and add the chickpeas, cumin, and salt. Season with black pepper.

2. Mix rice, sweet onion- chickpea combination, dates, chopped mint, and parsley in a big bowl. Mix well until combined. Serve warm-add vinaigrette if desired.

#30 EGG SALAD SANDWICH

Eggs are a perfect food for weight watchers. They are very tasty and balanced in calories and contain sufficient protein for a healthy meal.

- Yield: 4 servings

Ingredients:

- 6 hard- boiled eggs, chopped
- 1/3 cup low-fat mayo
- 2 sweet onions, minced
- 1/4 teaspoon curry powder
- 2 tsp. mustard(yellow or Dijon)
- 2-3 tsp. sweet pickle relish
- 1 teaspoon paprika
- 1/8 tea spoons crushed pepper
- ¼ tsp. salt

Preparation:

1. Mix eggs, mayo, onions, curry powder, mustard, pickle relish, paprika, pinch of salt, and pepper, in a bowl; mix well.

2. Can serve on bread or crackers.

#31 CHICKPEA SLAW

You can prepare this for your weekend lunch or any weekend outing.

- Prep Time: 10 minutes
- Yield: Makes 2 servings

Ingredients:

- 1/4 cup fat-free yogurt (plain)
- 1 tablespoon apple cider vinegar
- 1 tablespoon water
- 1/4 teaspoon salt
- ground black pepper
- 1 15oz. can chickpeas, drained and rinsed
- 2 1/2 cups cut green cabbage
- 2 stalks celery, finely sliced
- 2 carrots, thinly sliced and peeled
- 2 tablespoons toasted sesame seeds

Preparation:

1. In a middle bowl, mix the plain yogurt, vinegar, water, pinch of salt, and pepper to taste. Add the chickpeas, cabbage, celery,

and carrots; toss the ingredients. Cover with toasted sesame seeds.

2. Put the slaw in a storage bag or container. Chill minimum 4 hours before you serve; it can keep up to 3-4 days.

#32 LENTIL SOUP WITH TOASTED PITAS

This bean soup is a hearty, fiber rich meal that is delicious anytime of the year. Beans are a great source of fiber and protein.

- Cook Time: 20 minutes
- Yield: 4 servings

Ingredients:

- 1 table spoon extra-virgin olive oil
- 2 carrots, chopped
- 2 celery stalks, chopped
- 1 onion, chopped
- 2 garlic pieces, diced
- 1/2 teaspoons ground pepper
- 1/2 tea spoons salt
- 1/2 teaspoon crushed red pepper
- 8 cups water
- 1 cup dry lentils
- 2 tablespoons lemon juice
- 4 whole-grain pitas, and toasted

Preparation:

1. Heat oil in a big pot over medium heat. Add the celery, carrots, slice onions, chopped garlic, crushed red pepper, salt, and pepper; cook 4- 5 minutes.

2. Add the water and lentils. Reduce heat to low and simmer, partly covered, about 15 minutes.

3. Using a hand-held blender or masher, puree soup until partly smooth.

4. Sprinkle with lemon juice; serve with the toasted pitas.

#33 WHITE CHICKEN CHILE

This is a quick recipe that tastes as if it simmered all day! Using rotisserie chicken from the grocery saves much time on those busy nights.

Servings: 8

Cook Time: 15-20 minutes

Ingredients:

- 2 cans(15.5oz) white chili beans, drained
- 1 can (10oz.) diced tomatoes and green chilies ,undrained
- 1 can (14oz) reduced sodium chicken broth
- 1 can cream of chicken soup
- 1-2 jalapenos, seeded and diced
- 1 cooked rotisserie chicken from grocery
- Dash of hot sauce, to taste
- 1 tsp. lemon juice

Preparation:

1. Add 1 ½ cans of white chili beans to a large stock pot. Mash the remaining ½ can chili beans with fork and add to the pot.

2. Add the rest of ingredients to the pot.

3. Bring to a boil; then reduce heat and simmer 15 minutes, stirring occasionally.

4. Top with sour cream, cheese or tortilla strips.

#34 OLD FASHIONED NO-BAKE COOKIES

Dark chocolate with oats is a healthy recipe your kids will love!

- Yield: 4 servings

Ingredients:

- 2 tablespoons peanut butter
- 2 tablespoon low-fat milk
- 1/4 cup semi-sweet chocolate chips
- 3/4 cup rolled oats

Preparation:

1. Heat the peanut butter, low-fat milk, and chocolate chips in pan on low heat for 3- 4 minutes or till the chips become melted.

2. Add in the oats. Stir and remove from heat.

3. With a spoon or with a little ice cream scoop, make ball-shaped slices on wax paper. Cool in fridge for 10 minutes.

#35 EGG AND RICE SALAD

This recipe is very delicious, easy to prepare and popular at picnics.

- Prep Time: minutes
- Yield: Makes 12 servings

Ingredients

- 3 cups prepared brown rice
- 10 oz. package of frozen peas
- 1 cup celery, diced
- ¼ cup onion-diced
- 8 hard-boiled eggs, chopped
- ½ cup Monterey jack cheese, cubed
- 2 tablespoons pimentos
- 1 cup low-fat mayo
- 1-2 tbsp. yellow mustard(or Dijon)
- 1 tablespoon lemon juice
- 1 teaspoon salt
- ½ tsp. ground pepper
- 1/8 tsp dill
- 1 tablespoon paprika

Preparation

1. Rinse the frozen peas under cold water until separated; drain excess water.

2. In large bowl add together peas, eggs, rice, celery, onion, cheese, pimento.

3. In small bowl combine mayo, mustard, lemon juice, dill, and salt and pepper.

4. Sprinkle with paprika.

5. Cover and refrigerate until ready to serve.

53727038R00041

Made in the USA
San Bernardino, CA
26 September 2017